THIS BOOK
BELONGS TO:

PLEASE RETURN WITH CARE.

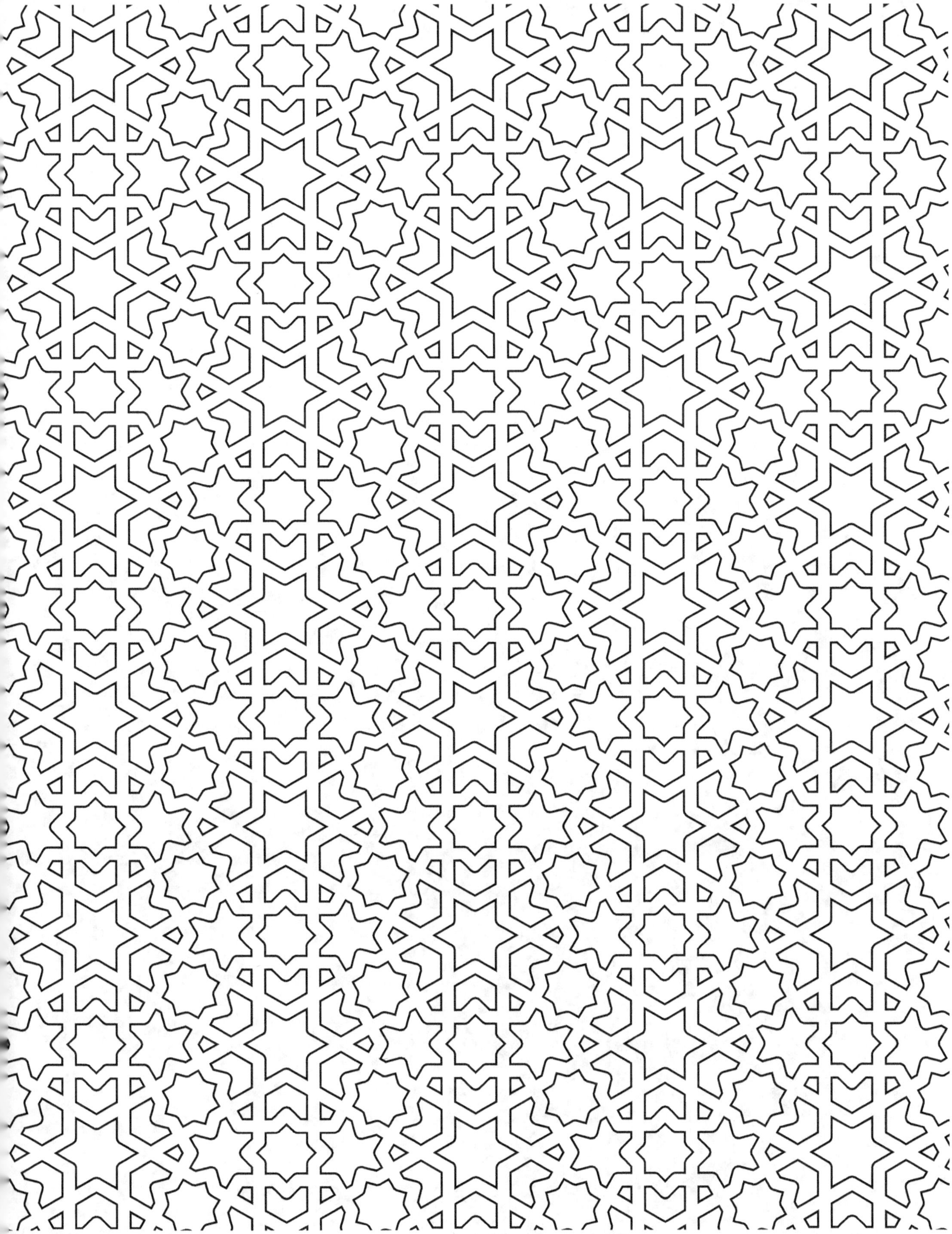

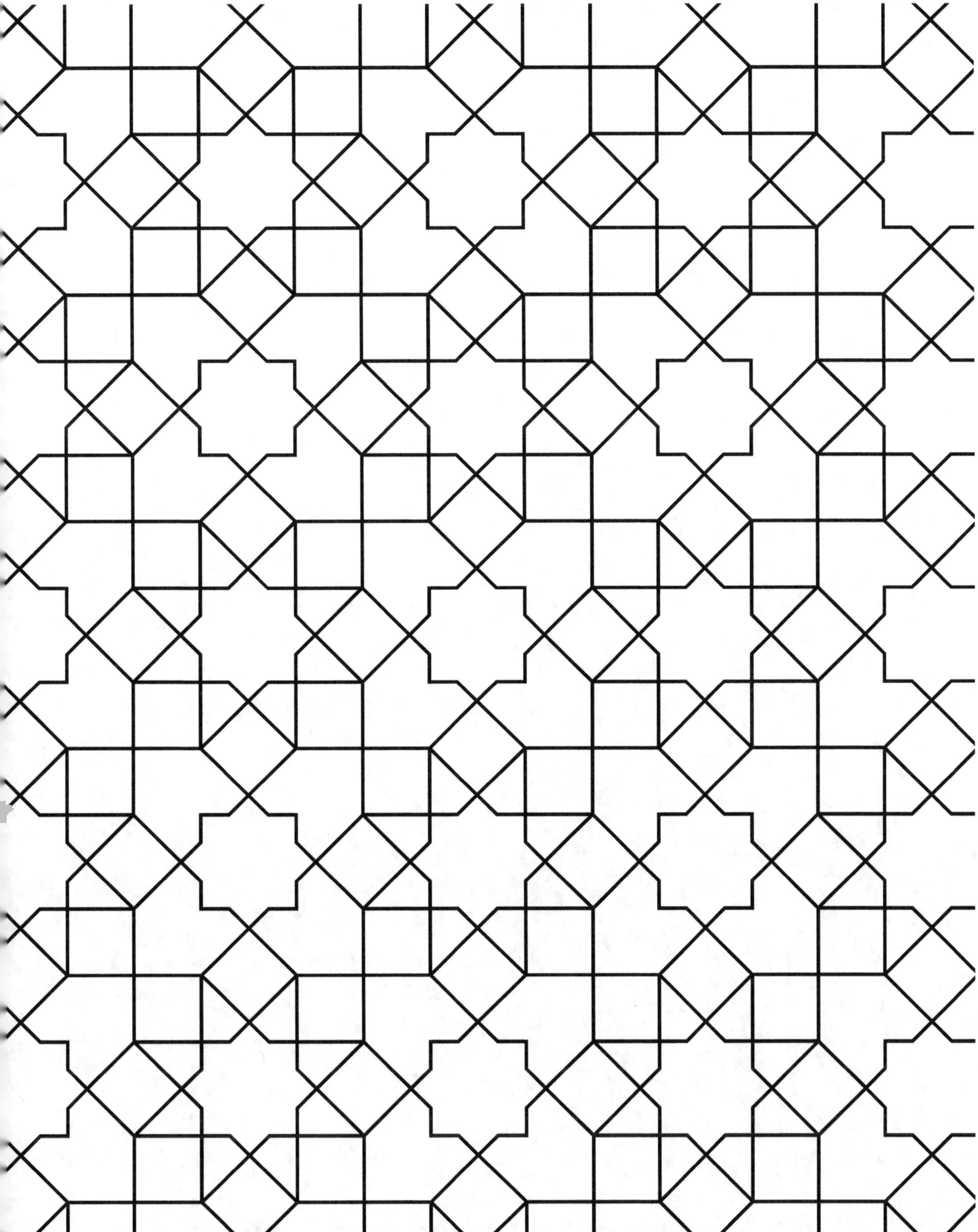

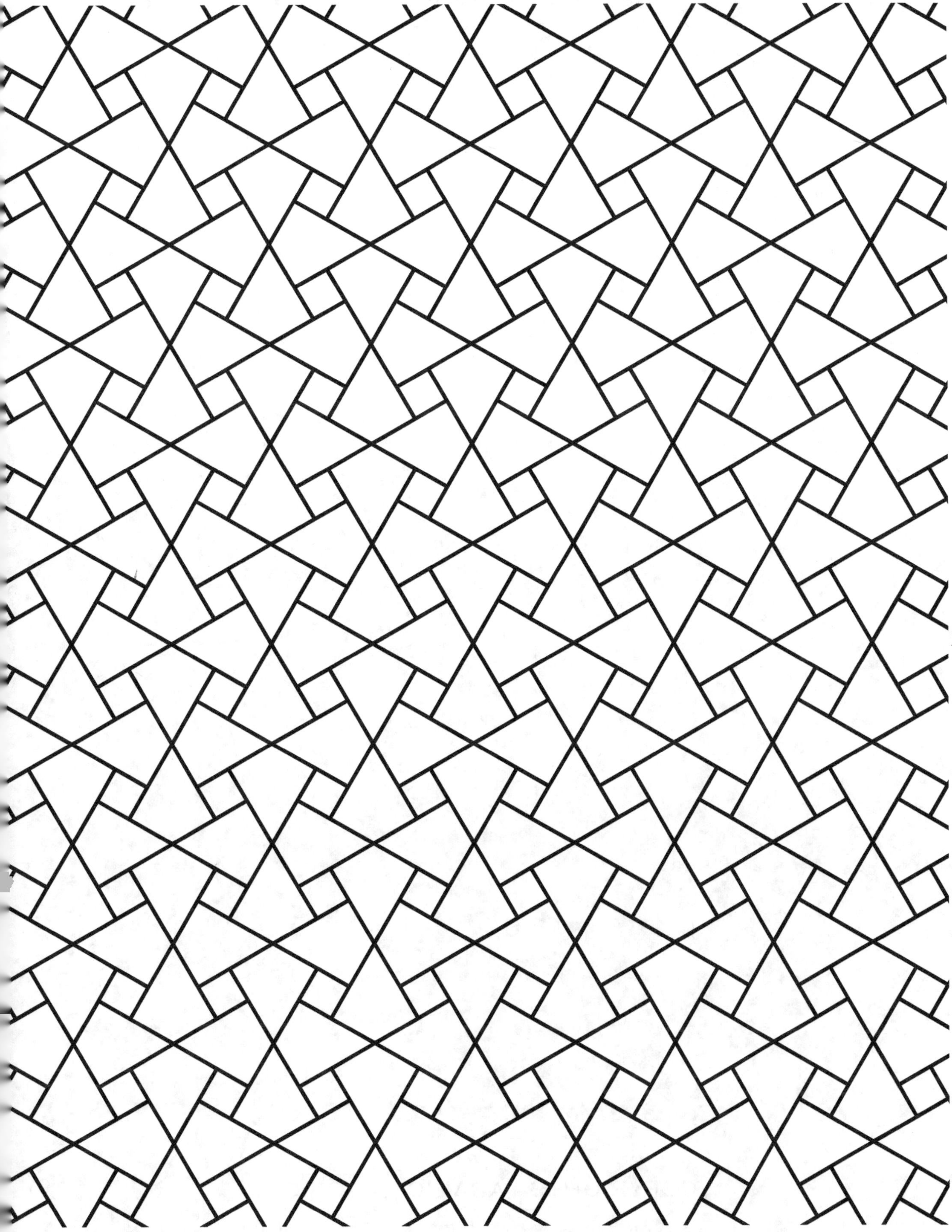

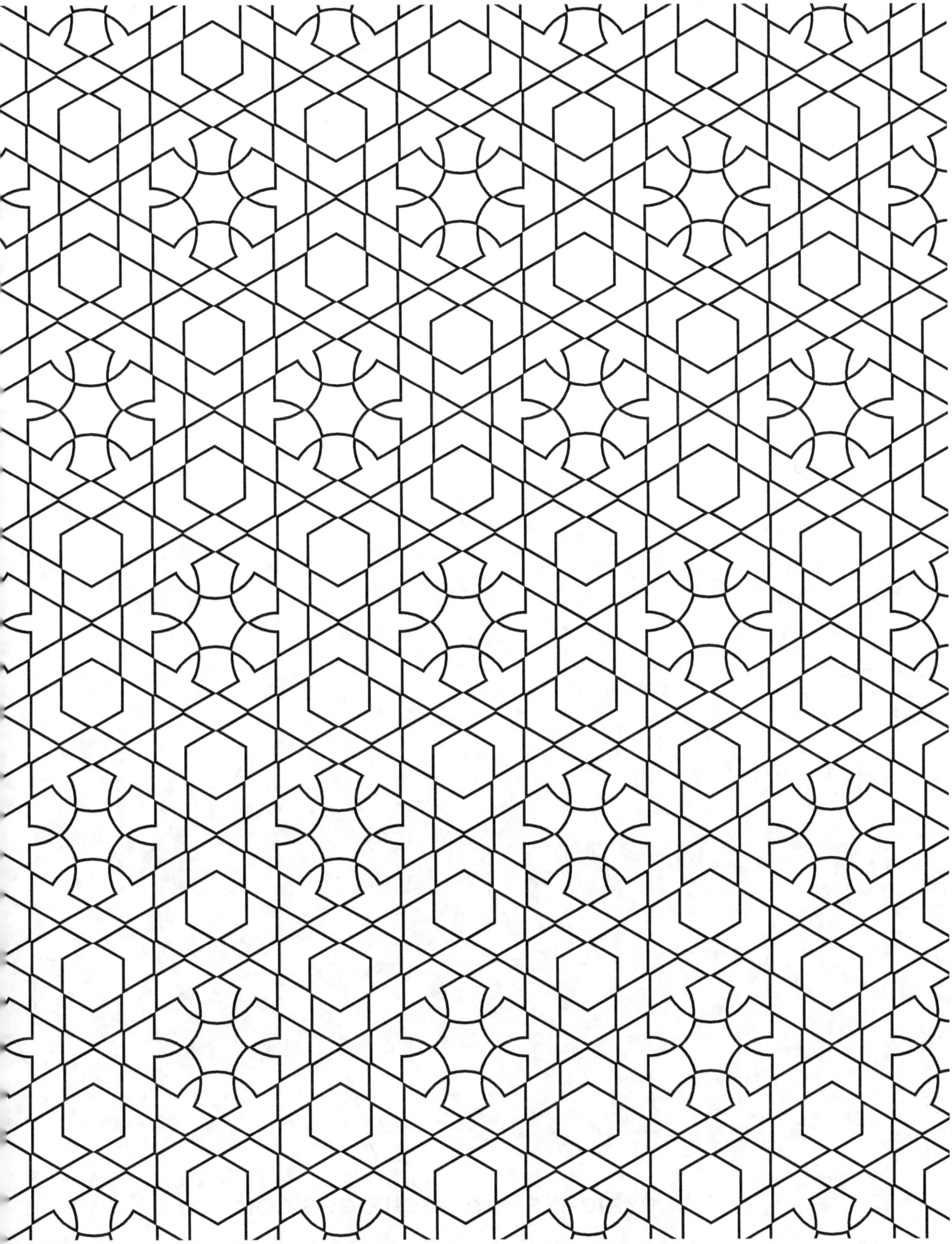

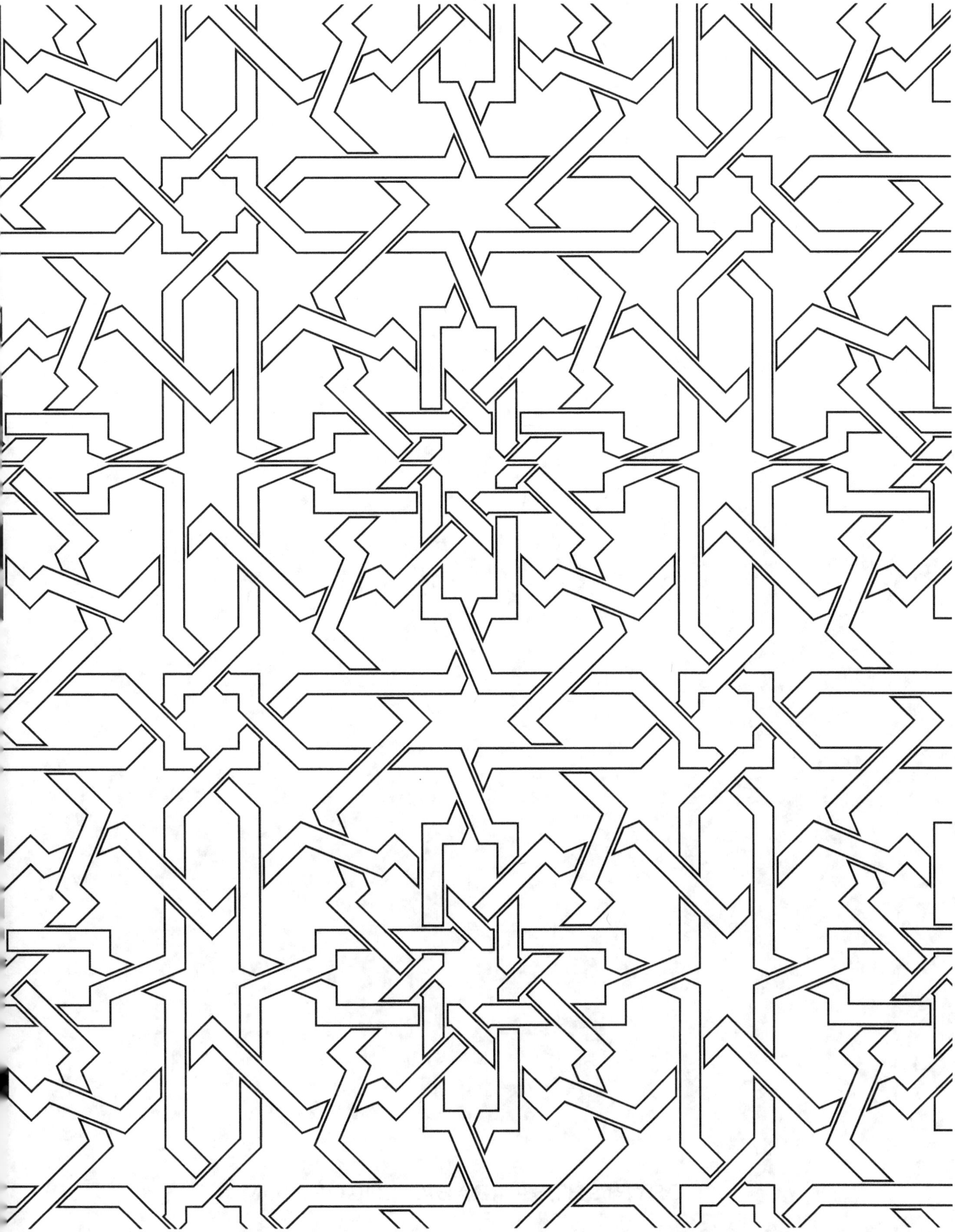

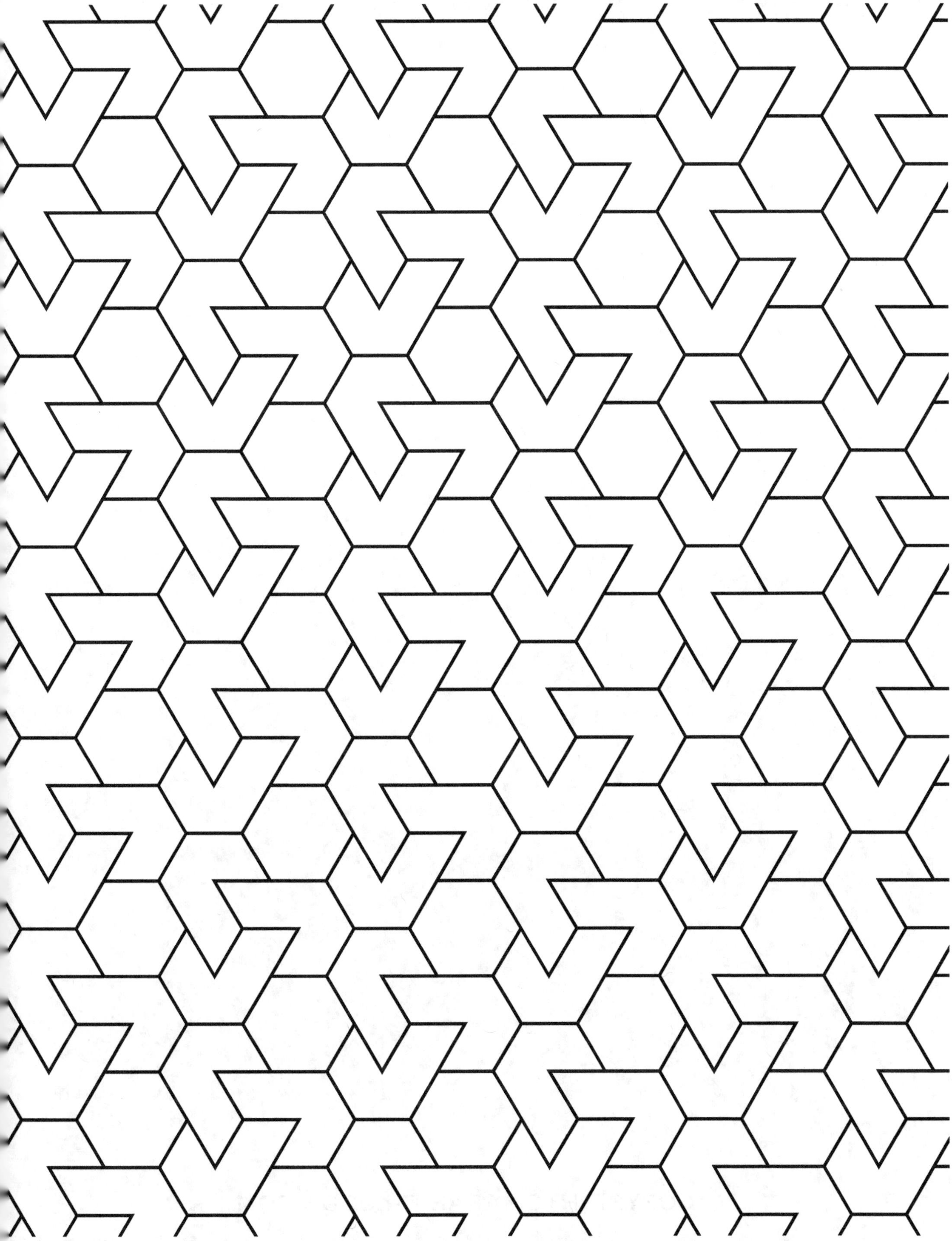

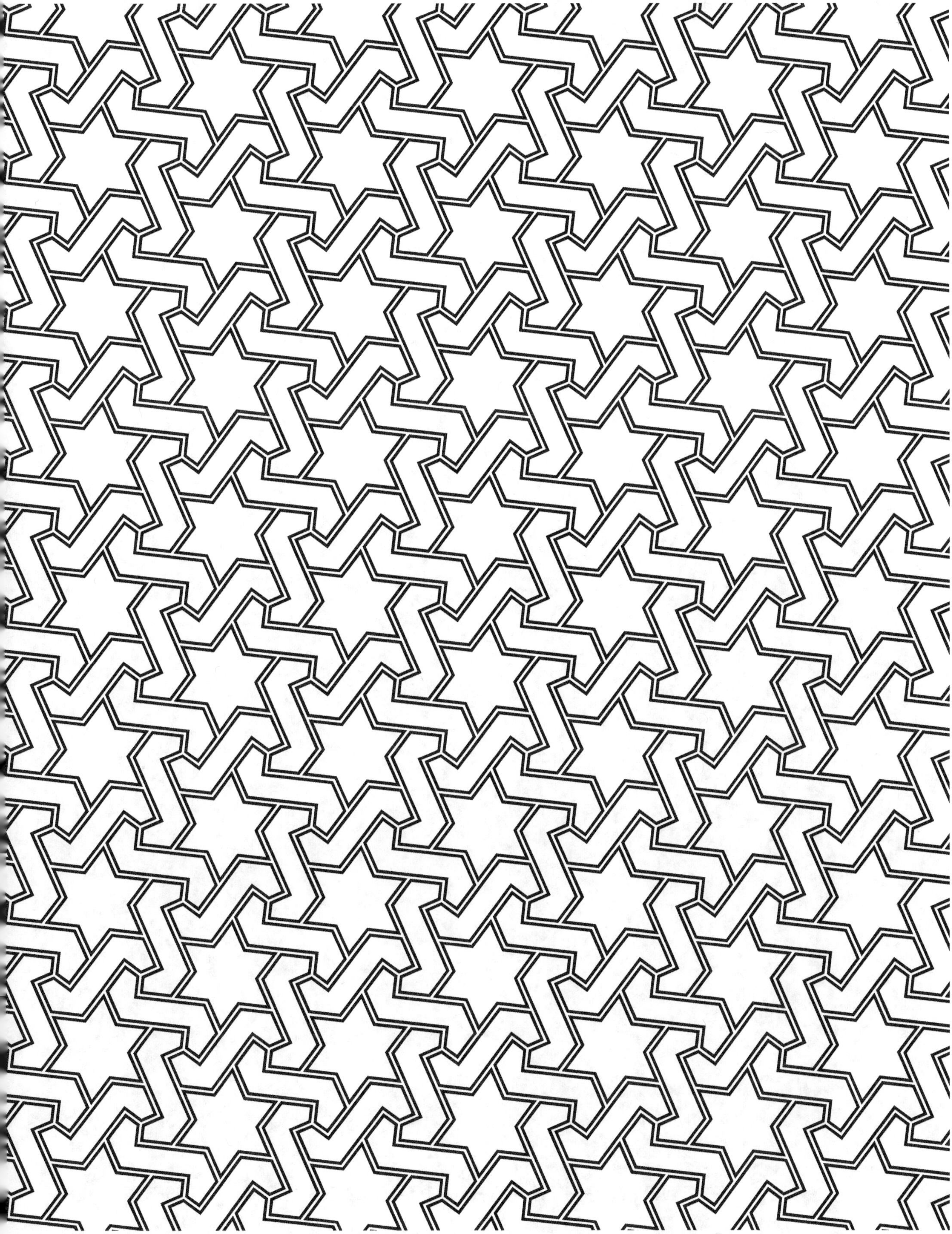

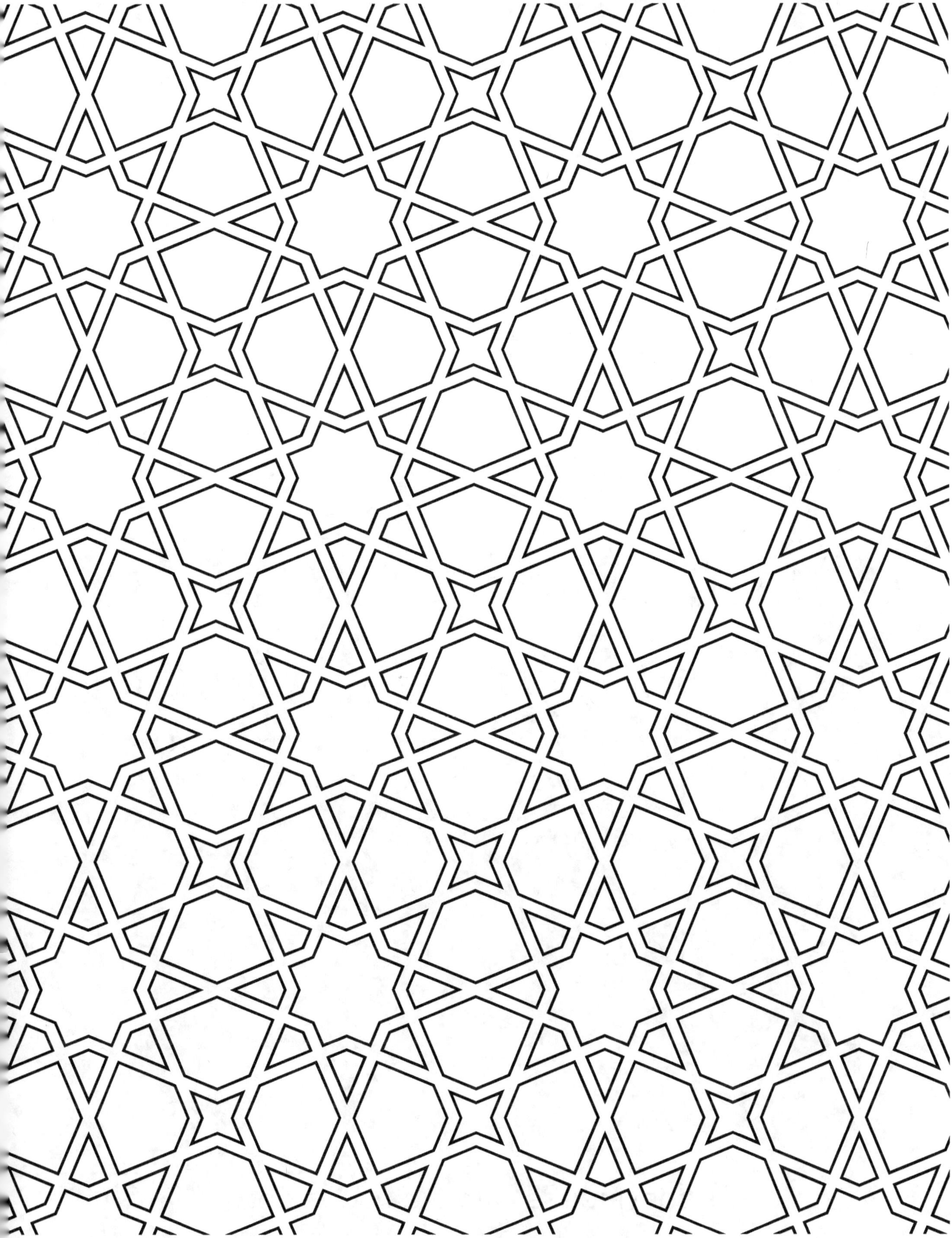

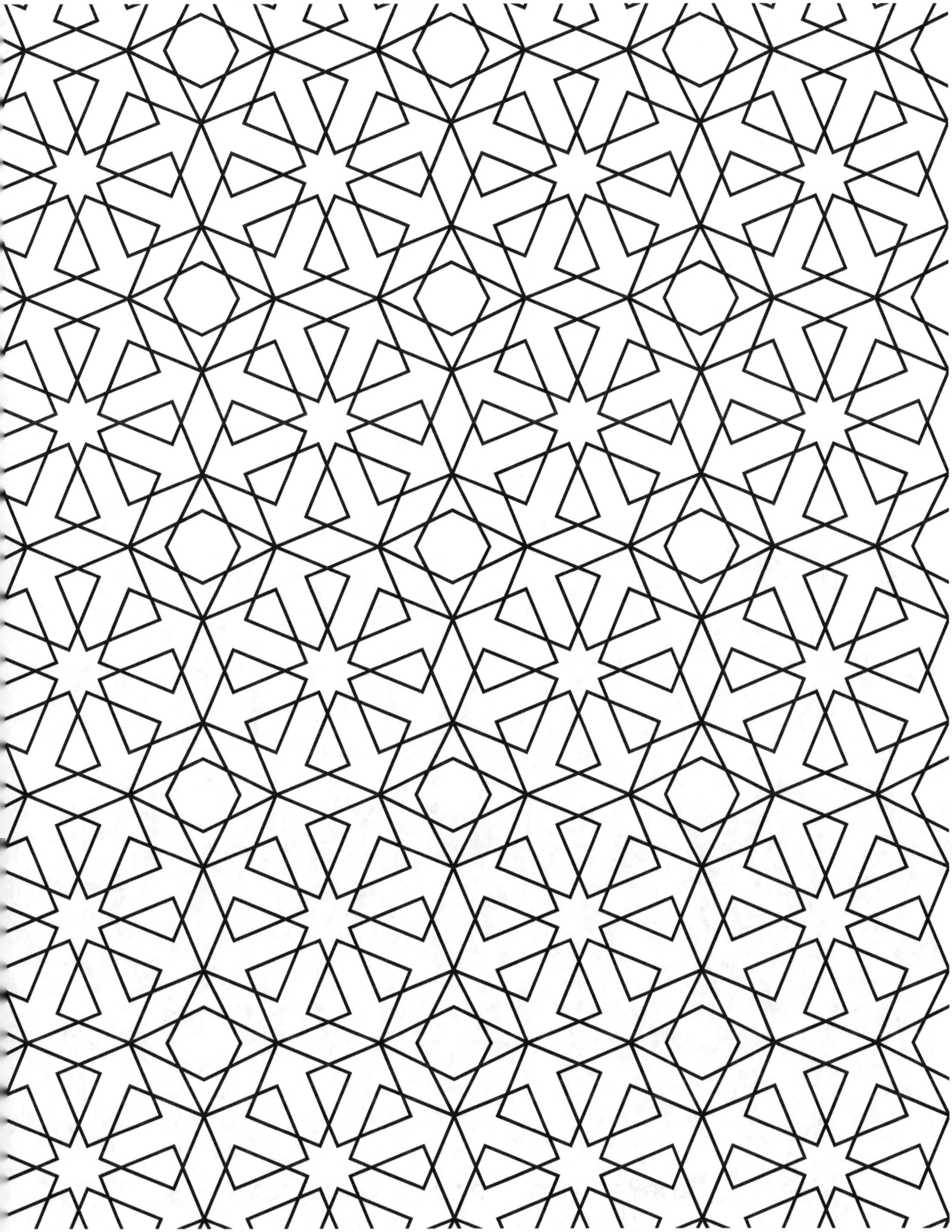

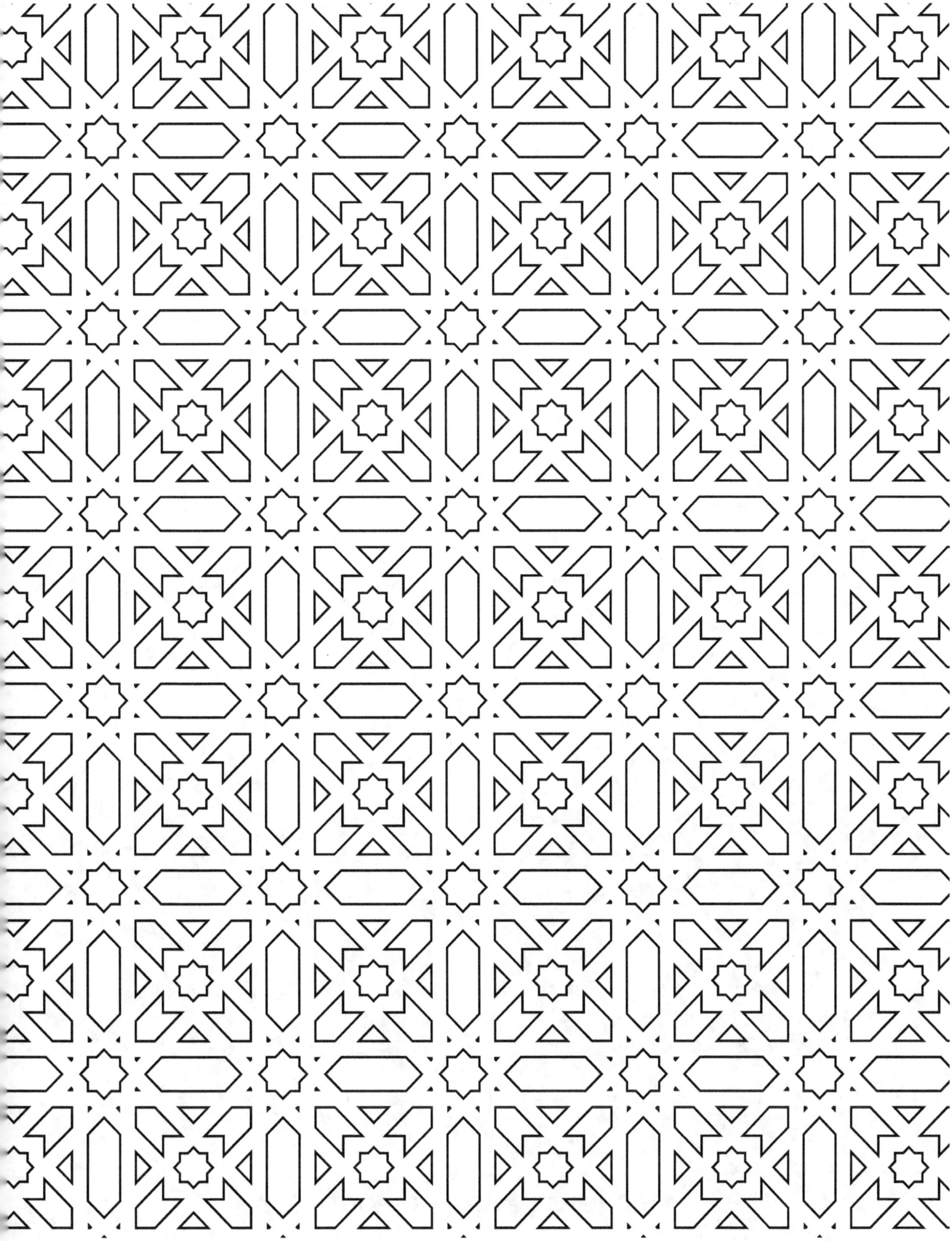

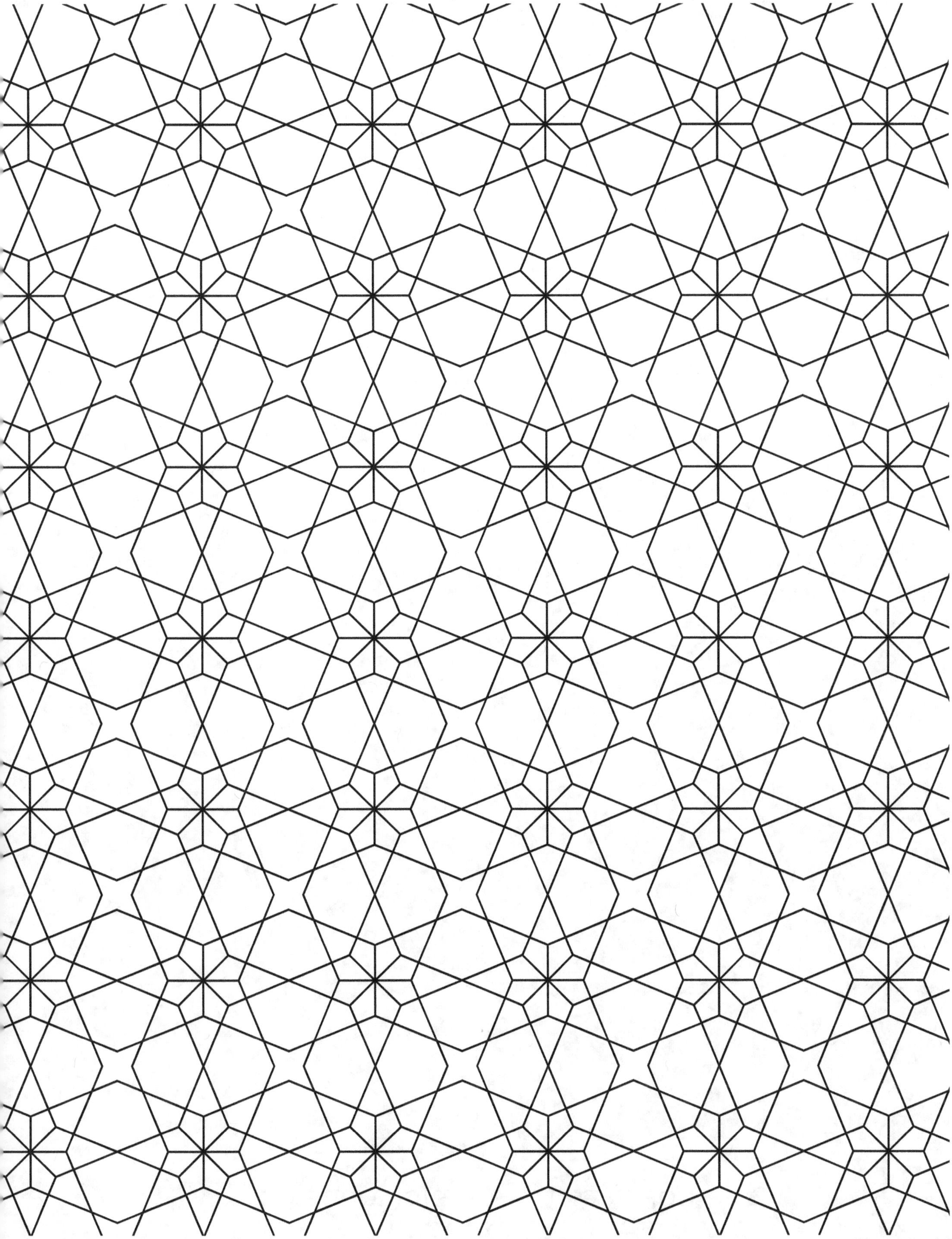

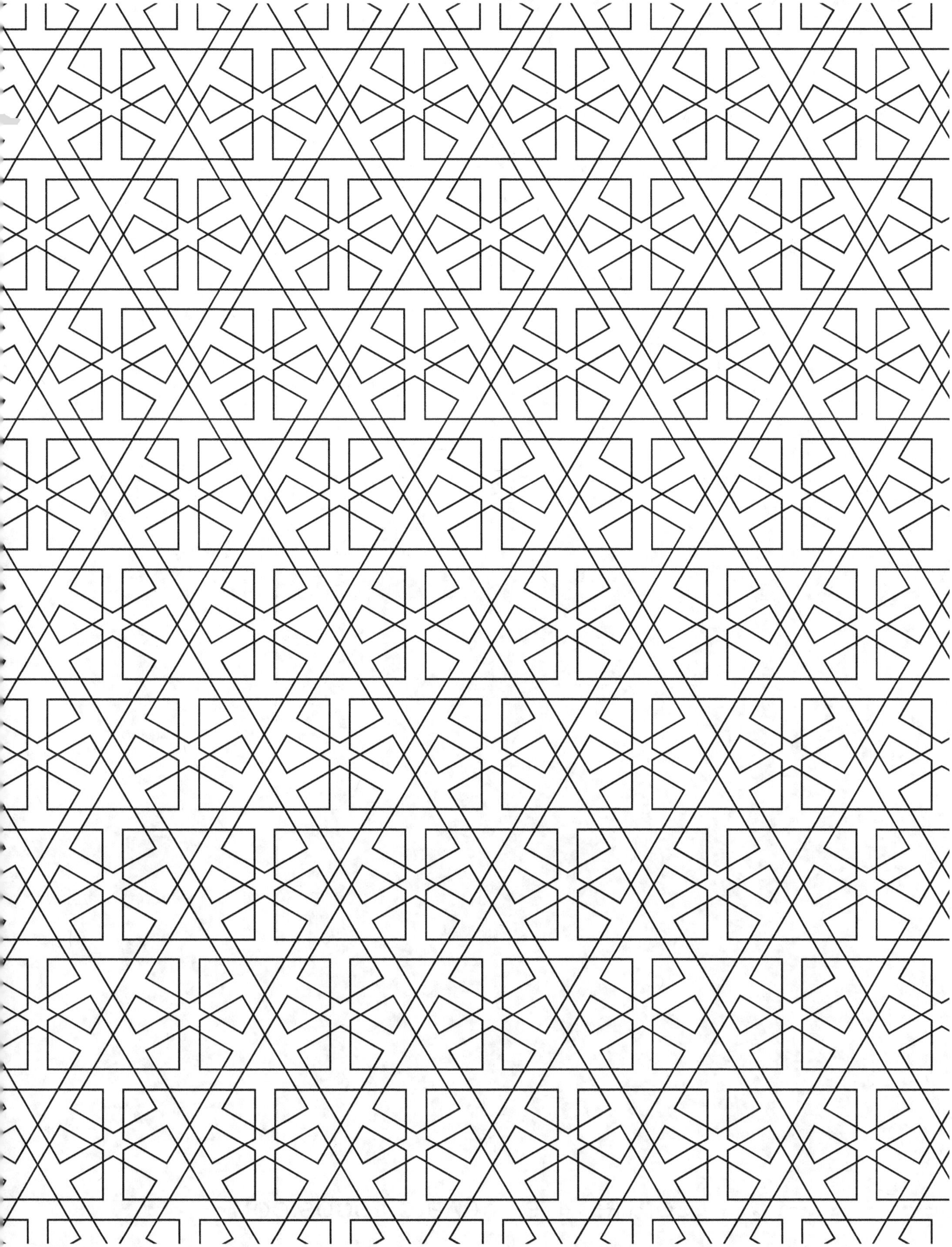

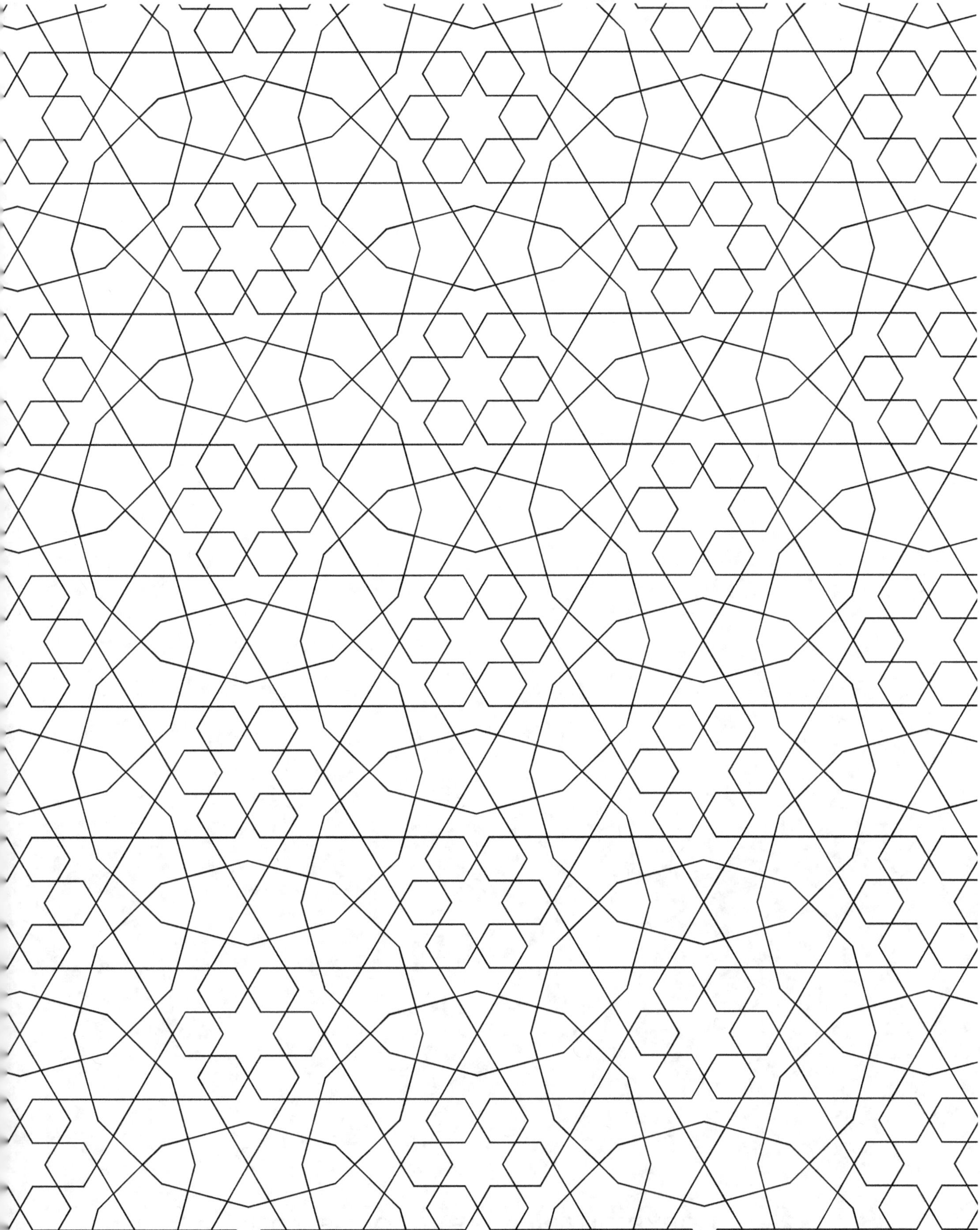

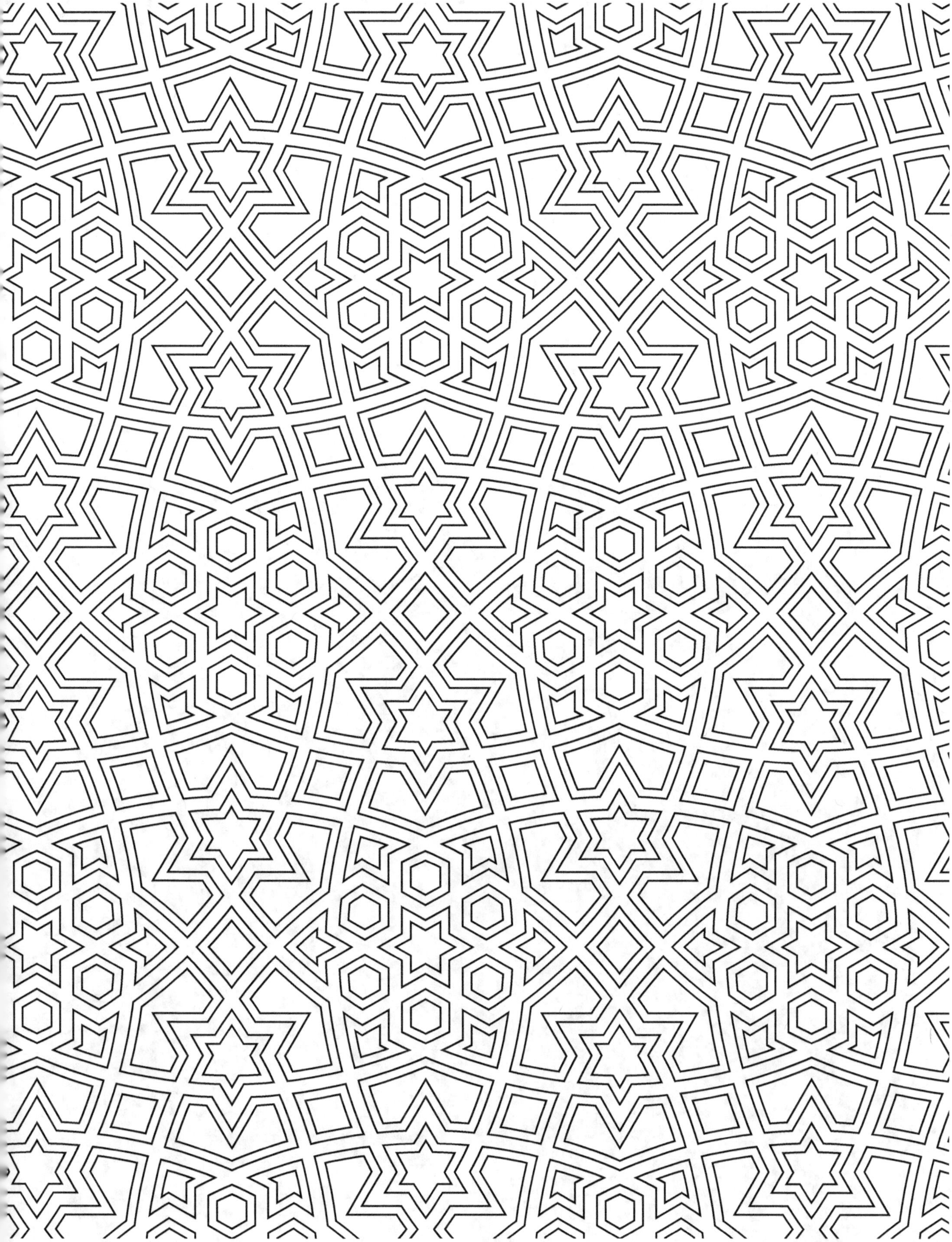

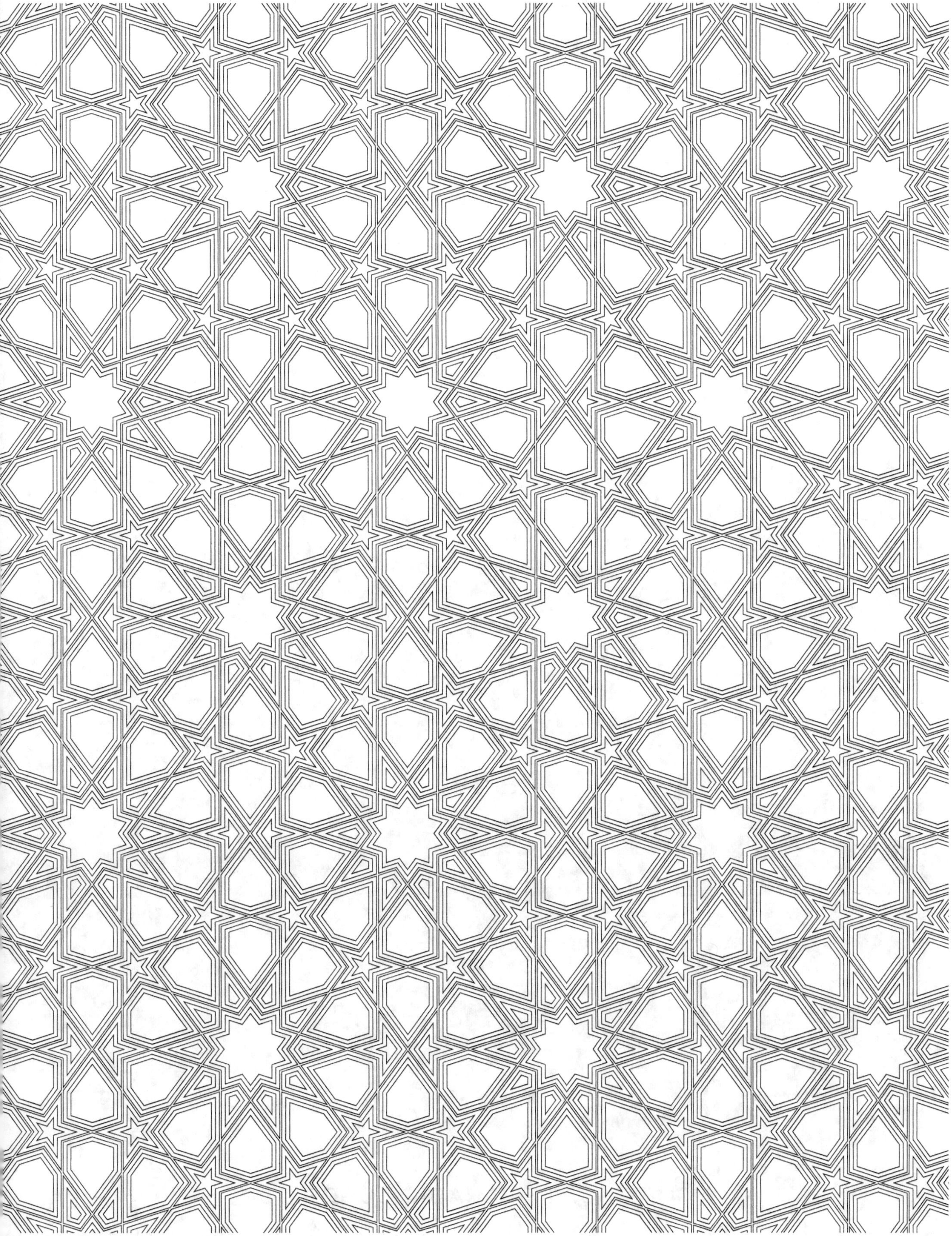

www.ingramcontent.com/pod-product-compliance
Lightning Source LLC
Chambersburg PA
CBHW081421220526
45467CB00009B/2779
* 9 7 9 8 7 2 6 7 0 3 2 4 4 *